The Kingfisher & other stories

Stephen Brock
Anne Vaughan

Cornelsen

The Kingfisher & other stories

Im Auftrage des Verlages erarbeitet von
Stephen Brock und Anne Vaughan

Beratende Mitwirkung und Übungen zu den Texten
Prof. Dr. Liesel Hermes, Karlsruhe

Grafik
Roy Schofield, Cheam

Umschlagfoto
Biofotos, Farnham, Surrey

2. Auflage Druck 6 5 4 Jahr 99 98

Alle Drucke dieser Auflage können im Unterricht nebeneinander verwendet werden.

Druck: Adolph Fürst & Sohn, Berlin

ISBN 3-464-05853-0

Bestellnummer 58530

gedruckt auf säurefreiem Papier, umweltschonend hergestellt aus chlorfrei gebleichten Faserstoffen

Contents

The Kingfisher*

It was August and Jessica Jones was going on holiday with her friend Chris Wentworth and his parents. They were going to spend two weeks at Sutton near the Norfolk coast. The two children didn't look out of the windows much on the journey. They were busy in the back of the car. They were looking at maps of the Norfolk Broads*. They were reading books about the birds there. They were checking their telescopes*. The Norfolk coast and the Broads were great for bird-watchers and Jessica and Chris were looking forward to their holiday there. In Norfolk, Chris and Jessica spent all their time outside. There were lots of places that they wanted to visit and travelling was easy for them. Drivers always stopped for the two young bird-watchers with their telescopes and cameras. They never waited long. The coast was full of other bird-watchers, too. Chris and Jessica met them on the roads, in the nature reserves*, everywhere.

On the fifth day of the holiday, they left in the morning for Breydon Water, near Great Yarmouth. Mr and Mrs Wentworth were still having breakfast. The weather was warm and sunny. Jessica and Chris waited for ten minutes on the A 149 road. Then a car stopped for them and 45 minutes later they were walking along the path* at Breydon Water. There were birds in, on and over the water* and others that walked on the mud. Chris and Jessica watched them with their telescopes. The time passed* quickly. Later, when they were walking back to the road, they met two older bird-watchers.

"What have you seen today?" asked Jessica.

"Oh, we've seen a bittern*," answered the taller of the two young men.

"Great!" said Chris.

"And we saw some spoonbills* on Hickling Broad yesterday."

"Spoonbills? Really?" Jessica was surprised*. "We didn't see any."

"Well, they were there yesterday. Perhaps they're still there now."

Hickling Broad was only about 2 miles from Sutton. Chris and Jessica decided* to walk there the next morning. Spoonbills didn't visit this part of England very often and they really wanted to see them.

"I hope they're still there," said Jessica to her friend when they got to the village of Hickling Green.

"I'm sure they will be there," answered Chris. But it was a bad day for them. They spent four hours in the nature reserve in two different bird hides*. But they didn't see the spoonbills. They felt tired and disappointed and they still had to* walk home. They decided to take a different path back to Hickling Green. After a few minutes Jessica suddenly stopped.

"Look!" she said to Chris and pointed. "A kingfisher." The beautiful blue bird was standing* near the path.

"We've never been this near to a kingfisher before," said Chris. "They always fly away."

The two bird-watchers moved slowly nearer the kingfisher. It watched them but it still didn't fly away.

"What's wrong with it?" asked Jessica.

Very slowly they moved nearer and nearer and then stopped. The bird was only a metre away from them now. They looked at each other.

"Perhaps it's just tired," said Chris.

"Or ill," said Jessica. The bird didn't move. The two children got nearer to the kingfisher. They looked at it for a long time but couldn't see what was wrong. At last Chris decided to make a nest for it.

"But kingfishers don't make nests, Chris," said Jessica.

"I know," answered Chris, "but we've got to do something. It won't live long on the path." They quickly found some broken reeds* and Chris made a small, comfortable nest near some bushes. Then they went back to the path and Jessica picked up* the kingfisher.

"Poor bird," she said and touched the kingfisher's blue head*. It trembled*. Jessica carried it to the nest and put it in. The nest was just right. "Very nice," said Jessica. "And nobody can see you there. You're safe* till tomorrow."

"Well, what now?" asked Chris.

"Let's talk to the warden* at the nature reserve tomorrow morning," said Jessica, and Chris agreed. They said 'Goodbye' to the kingfisher and walked back to Sutton.

The next morning they looked for the warden at his office in the nature reserve. The office opened at 9 o'clock but the warden wasn't there. They went to the road again and saw a group of young children.

"Have you seen the warden?" shouted Chris.

One of the group answered, "He's showing some tourists the nature reserve. He isn't coming back till one o'clock."

It was only eleven now, so Chris and Jessica decided to look for the kingfisher first.

"I hope it's all right," said Jessica when they saw the bushes. It was still there. The kingfisher sat in the nest and watched them.

They looked at the bird and then Jessica picked it up again. It trembled for a few minutes but then it was quite happy in the girl's hands.

"I think it likes me," she said to Chris. "You like me, don't you, King?"

"King?" asked Chris.

"Yes, that's his name. King the kingfisher."

"You like me, don't you, King?" said another voice* suddenly. Chris and Jessica looked back and saw the group of children from the warden's office again. There were four of them, all about 12 years old, two boys and two girls.

"What have you got there?" asked the tall boy.

Jessica smiled. "A kingfisher. Isn't it lovely?" She showed the small bird to the group of children.

"Isn't it lovely?" said the tall boy and the others all laughed.

"Give it to us," said the other boy in the group. "We can have some fun with it. Can't it fly?"

"Yes," said the tall boy. "Come on, give it to us. It doesn't belong to* you."

"Oh, go away! Don't be so silly. This is a nature reserve," said Chris.

"The animals don't belong to anybody." Jessica helped him. "Yes, you mustn't disturb* the animals and birds here. Ask the warden."

"Well, you're disturbing them, aren't you?" said the tall boy. "The warden isn't going to like that. Just wait. We're going to tell* him."

"Come on, Jessica, let's go," said Chris to his friend. "I don't want to talk to these silly, little* children."

The two bird-watchers walked away along the path. The group of children laughed and the tall boy shouted, "We're going to tell the warden." Then one of the two girls said, "Come on, they're boring. We don't want their silly bird."

Chris and Jessica were very worried*. Were they doing the right thing? "Perhaps those children are right," said Jessica. "If we tell the warden, he'll be angry." They made a new nest for the kingfisher in a different place. Jessica thought the bird wasn't frightened of them any more. But they couldn't give it any fish.

"If it doesn't eat," said Chris, "it will die* soon. We've got to tell the warden." So the next morning they walked to Hickling Green again and found the warden in his office. He was a big, friendly man with a nice smile. He listened to Chris and Jessica. Then he explained, "Well, your kingfisher is probably ill. We usually* leave them alone when they're ill. We don't look after them like people, you know. But let's go and look at it. Come on." Chris and Jessica took him quickly to the bird's nest.

"It's there." Jessica pointed to the bushes. The nest was there. But there wasn't a kingfisher in it.

"Oh, no!" Jessica was very upset*. "Those terrible children. They've found it."

"Perhaps it's here somewhere," said the warden. "Let's look for it." For ten minutes they looked for the kingfisher in the reeds and bushes. But they couldn't find King anywhere. Jessica felt really sad and Chris was upset, too.

"Perhaps King just flew away," he said. "Perhaps he's all right now." They started to walk away. Jessica looked at the path and thought about the kingfisher. Poor King! So beautiful and now he was dead*. She was sure of that. She was still thinking this when Chris suddenly shouted, "Look! Up there*!" On the top of a tall tree* sat a beautiful, blue kingfisher.

"It's King. I know it is. King!" Jessica shouted. "You're all right again." Chris wasn't so sure. There were lots of kingfishers in the Norfolk Broads. They all looked the same to him. But Jessica was sure. The warden smiled.

"Well done, you two," he said. "If that's King, he's fine now. You've done a great job."

Suddenly, the kingfisher flew back up the path. Jessica ran after it. Then Chris and the warden came, too. The little bird flew to the nest in the bushes. When Chris and Jessica arrived, it just sat and looked at them.

"I think you're right," said Chris. He was sure now, too. The kingfisher was in the nest. It wasn't frightened of them.

"It's King." They watched the bird for a few minutes. Suddenly it flew over Jessica's head and then back to the nest. Then it flew out again and disappeared* into the reeds of Hickling Broad. This time it didn't come back.

When the warden said 'Goodbye', Chris and Jessica stood* and watched the reeds for a few minutes more. They felt sad that King was gone* now. Then Jessica said to her friend, "Chris, it's sad, isn't it? But it's great that he's safe now. I'm so glad we saved him, aren't you?"

p. 4 kingfisher = *Eisvogel*; Broads = *Seenplatte*; telescope = *Fernglas*; nature reserve = *Naturschutzgebiet*
p. 5 path = *Pfad, Weg*; water = *Wasser*; pass (v) = *vergehen*; bittern = *Rohrdommel*; spoonbill = *Löffler, Löffelreiher*; surprised = *überrascht;* decide (v) = *beschließen*; bird hide = *Versteck zum Beobachten von Vögeln*; had to = *mußten*
p. 6 stand (v) = *stehen*; reed = *Schilf*; pick up (v) = *aufheben*; head = *Kopf*; tremble (v) = *zittern*; safe = *sicher*; warden = *Wächter*
p. 7 voice = *Stimme;* belong to (v) = *gehören*
p. 8 disturb (v) = *stören*; tell (v) = *erzählen*; little = *klein;* worried = *besorgt;* die (v) = *sterben;* usually = *gewöhnlich*
p. 9 upset = *verstört;* dead = *tot;* up there = *da oben;* tree = *Baum*
p. 10 disappear (v) = *verschwinden;* stood (v) = *stand(en)*; gone = *weg*

The hard way up*

"I can't walk any more," said Barry.

"It isn't far now. Come on," said Nicole but she stopped and waited for him. Sonia and Jed, who were with Nicole, waited, too. The other two teams walked on and soon disappeared. The twelve people in the group – all members of the Gateway Youth Club in Manchester – were on a ten-day survival* holiday in Snowdonia National Park, North Wales.

Three of them, Nicole, Clive and another boy, were over eighteen and they were the team leaders. These team leaders had to know about survival skills* and each was a leader in a team of four. The others were from thirteen to sixteen years old and they were still at school. In their rucksacks, they were carrying tents* and other equipment*, warm clothes and some food.

Nicole, Sonia and Jed waited a minute for Barry. He was the smallest. Sonia and Jed were both bigger than him. Nicole was nineteen and the strongest* member of the team. A few minutes later, Nicole's team found the others.

"This is the best place for a camp*," said Clive. "There's water here and shelter* from the wind." Clive was the oldest and the leader of all three teams in the Gateway group. Some of the others were already making a camp fire*. Others were putting up* the green tents.

After the evening meal, Clive stood up and spoke to the big group.
"I just want to talk about the plans for the next two days," he said. "I've got a surprise for you. Tomorrow we're going to make camp near Snowdon." Some people cheered*. "That's about nine miles."
"Nine miles," Barry said to Nicole. "One mile in the mountains* feels like five miles on flat ground*." Nicole smiled.
"And on Tuesday," Clive went on, "we're going to climb the south side* of Snowdon. Now, some of you want to take photos of animals and plants tomorrow. That's fine, but please stay with your team. You don't want to get lost. It's very beautiful here, I know, but it can be dangerous in bad weather. So please remember – stay together."

That evening, everybody sat near the camp fire and sang. The songs went on till ten o'clock in the evening but that was too late for most people. At half-past nine, almost everybody was in bed. Sonia, Nicole, Barry and Jed were still sitting near the fire at ten past ten.They spoke quietly now.

"Why have we got to climb Snowdon?" said Barry. "My grandmother was on Snowdon last year. She went by train to the top." Sonia laughed.
"That's OK for your grandma," she said. "We want to go the hard way up."

"And," said Jed, "the train goes up the north side of the mountain. We're going to climb Snowdon from the south side. There isn't even a path there."

"I've never climbed a mountain before," said Barry. "What's it like?"

"It can be dangerous," said Nicole, "if the weather is bad and you do the wrong thing. But all the leaders have had survival training* and you've all learned survival skills from me. You'll have no problems." She smiled. "Just stay with me and you'll be OK." Barry was worried but he smiled at Nicole.

"Yes, Nicole. Thanks. I've always wanted to go on a survival holiday, but now I'm so near to the mountain, I'm not sure," he said. But after that, Sonia called him 'Grandma'.

It was cold at seven o'clock in the morning. Most of the group washed in the cold water from the river.

"It's cold enough for snow*," said Barry.

"Snow! Good," said Sonia. "It's more interesting like that, Grandma."

"Don't listen to her," said Nicole. "And don't worry! This is a holiday, remember?"

After breakfast at quarter to eight, the teams packed the equipment in their rucksacks. They started their day's journey, north from Porthmadog. Between* breakfast and twelve o'clock, they walked five miles. Everybody was hungry but happy. That afternoon, they wanted to travel another four miles.

"Oh, not another hill!" said Barry. "I've got pains in my legs and pains in my arms. What a place!"

"Come on, Grandma," said Sonia. "It's a lovely day for a little walk*." She laughed. Barry didn't think it was very funny. Nicole was carrying the tent equipment, but

Barry's rucksack felt really heavy*. They had to cross* a river. There wasn't a bridge, so they had to cross on stones*. The river was very deep* and Barry almost fell into the cold water and Nicole had to rescue* him. Sonia laughed and said, "You've already washed this morning, Grandma!" Sonia was making Barry angry.

At the end of the day, almost everybody was tired. They made camp near the mountain. Snowdon was blue and grey. There were no paths and no shelter. Barry was worried. "Can I climb it?" he thought. "I don't want to look silly in front* of the others. And not in front of Sonia."

In the morning, Clive spoke to them again.
"Remember, everybody, this is a nature reserve. Please leave fifteen minutes between teams," said Clive. "And please leave five metres between you and the boy or girl in front of you. If we all walk together, we'll disturb the plants on the mountain." Each team started at a different time. Nicole's team started last. The sun disappeared. It was getting colder and darker. There wasn't a path and the team had to walk between big stones. Barry climbed slowly. Soon, there was no sign of the other teams.
Sonia called to Jed and Barry, "Come on, Jed. Hurry up, Grandma!" She climbed onto a big stone and jumped. Then she screamed*. The others ran to Sonia. She was on the ground. "My ankle! Oh!" Sonia screamed.
"Don't move," said Nicole. She felt Sonia's ankle.
"Stop that!" said Sonia. "That hurts*."
"You haven't broken it. You've just got a sprained ankle," said Nicole. "Can you stand up?" Jed and Barry helped Sonia to stand.
"I can try," she said. She tried, but it wasn't any good. Then it started to snow.

"Sit there for a minute," said Nicole.

"What are we going to do?" asked Jed.

"Can you carry her rucksack? Barry and I can try to help Sonia," said Nicole. But Jed couldn't carry both rucksacks. They were too heavy. Nicole and Barry helped Sonia to stand. She tried but she couldn't walk. She was in pain.

"It isn't any good," she said. "I can't do it. Are you sure it isn't broken?"

"I'm not sure," said Nicole. "Now listen to me, everybody," she said. "There's going to be a snowstorm and Sonia can't walk." The others looked at her. "Somebody has got to stay here with Sonia," said Nicole.

"I'll stay," said Barry. He didn't know why he said it. The words just came out.

"Thanks, Barry," said Nicole. "Jed and I will go for help. OK?" They all agreed.

"First, we have got to put up a tent for Sonia and Barry," said Nicole.

Snow was falling quickly now. "You've got to have shelter," explained Nicole. "If you haven't, this snow can kill* you in a few hours." They put up the tent and tied* the tent ropes* on to some bushes. It was difficult in the snow and they worked for a long time. Nicole found a survival blanket* for Sonia and Barry, then she and Jed helped Sonia into the tent. "Now listen. Jed and I are going up to the restaurant at the top of the mountain. They've got a phone there and we can get help. Stay together in the tent. Don't go out into the snow." She put the rucksacks in front of the tent, Nicole and Jed started up the mountain. The snow was falling fast and in a few minutes they disappeared.

Barry and Sonia felt very alone. The wind was coming into the tent.

"I'm cold," said Sonia. They sat together and trembled in the cold. Sonia tried to get comfortable but the pain in her ankle was too much for her. It was getting colder and colder in the tent. "How long ago did Nicole and Jed leave?" she asked.

"Only an hour," answered Barry.

"What's the time now?" she asked.

"Four-thirty," said Barry.

"When does it get dark?" asked Sonia.

"In an hour," said Barry. "Perhaps sooner in this snowstorm. Don't worry. I'm sure they're at the top now." He spoke in a confident* voice, but he was worried really. "Who can help us? Can they rescue people in snowstorms?" he thought, but he didn't say anything.

The wind was pulling at the tent. Barry couldn't see the rucksacks outside. They were already under the snow. Suddenly, the rope broke and the tent fell on to them. They were both frightened and screamed, then Barry climbed out and moved away the snow which was on the tent. He put up the tent again.

"How can anybody find us now?" asked Sonia.

"They know we're here," said Barry.

"I've never been so cold," said Sonia.

"Let's try to get warm," said Barry. But they couldn't get warm. "Why doesn't somebody come?" he thought. "Perhaps they're already looking for us and can't find us." Barry looked out. The snow was very deep. The next time he looked, it was dark outside.

They listened to the wind for a long time. Sonia and Barry were both cold and frightened. They didn't want to think about the snow outside, so they talked and talked. Sonia explained that she didn't really have any friends. She thought the others liked confident people and she wanted to make friends. So she tried to be confident in the team.

"But that was the wrong thing to do, wasn't it?" she said.

"Yes," said Barry. "You made me feel silly and that made me angry."

"I'm sorry I was mean* to you. And now you've been so nice to me. Thanks."

"Forget it," said Barry. Sonia thought Barry was really nice. She wanted to look at him but she couldn't see him in the dark tent. But then, suddenly, she could see Barry's head! Where was the light coming from?

"I've found them!" shouted a voice. "Here they are!" Somebody pulled back the tent. Sonia and Barry saw four

people with lights on their helmets* and a voice said, "Which of you has the sprained ankle?" Two people carried Sonia and they all started up the mountain.

In the restaurant at the top of Snowdon, Clive and the others were waiting. When Barry and Sonia came in, everybody cheered.

"Here you are," said Clive. "Have some tea and soup." The four people with the word 'Rescue' on their helmets smiled and had some tea, too.

"Thanks. Thank you, everybody," said Sonia. "And thank you, Barry." She kissed* him in front of all the others and Barry went red. "And next time we want to go up Snowdon," she said, "we can go by train!"

p. 11 the hard way up = *der schwierigste Aufstieg;* survival = *Überlebens-;* skill = *Fertigkeit;* tent = *Zelt;* equipment = *Ausrüstung;* the strongest = *der/die/das stärkste*
p. 12 camp = *Zeltlager;* shelter = *Schutz;* camp fire = *Lagerfeuer;* put up (v) = *aufbauen;* cheer (v) = *jubeln;* mountain = *Berg;* ground = *Boden;* south side = *Südseite*
p. 13 training = *Ausbildung;* snow = *Schnee;* between = *zwischen;* walk = *Spaziergang*
p. 14 heavy = *schwer;* cross (v) = *überqueren;* stone = *Stein;* deep = *tief;* rescue (v) = *retten;* in front of = *vor;* scream (v) = *schreien;* hurt (v) = *weh tun*
p. 15 kill (v) = *töten;* tie on (v) = *(fest)binden*
p. 16 rope = *Seil, Tau;* blanket = *Decke;* confident = *zuversichtlich, selbstbewußt*
p. 17 mean = *gemein*
p. 18 helmet = *Helm;* kiss (v) = *küssen*

Llanberis
Hebron Sta.
Halfway Sta.
Snowdon Mountain Railway
Clogwyn Sta.
Snowdon Summit Station
Mountain Rescue Post
Pass of Llanberis
Llyn Gwynant
Llyn Dinas
Beddgelert
Gelert's Grave
Pont Aber Glaslyn
River Glaslyn
Porthmadog

They aren't going to stop us

This diary* belongs to Karen Brennan. She lives in Coleraine, in Northern Ireland. Last summer she spent a holiday at Mourne Park camp at Kilkeel on the coast. Northern Ireland is a part of Britain but many Catholics* who live there want to belong to the Republic* of Ireland. The Protestants* have got different ideas. The two groups can't agree about what's best for Northern Ireland.

Sunday 5th August

I packed today. I can't wait for tomorrow. It's going to be great, great, great! I'm going to Kilkeel for two long weeks! I phoned Mary and Sharon and they're looking forward to it, too. The bus is leaving at nine. We arrive about twelve, in time for lunch*. Please, God*, don't let* it rain tomorrow. Make it warm and sunny. Please!

Monday 6th August

It rained all day. I've never seen a day so grey. I hope it isn't a bad sign. The bus was late, of course, and we had to wait in the rain for twenty minutes. Still, it was OK. Everybody was happy and we had a great time on the bus on the journey here. I sat next to Mary, and Sharon was next to Patrick McFee. I think she likes him. There were lots of cars and lorries on the roads and we didn't get to Kilkeel till after one o'clock. The last hour from Lisburn was beautiful, even in the rain. We were crossing the Mourne Mountains. We heard a song about them at school last month. I remember one part – "Where the Mountains o' Mourne sweep down* to the sea". It's a beautiful song.

The camp in Mourne Park, Kilkeel, is very nice, too. The beach* isn't very far away and the warden, Mr Kennedy, says that you can see the mountains most days. We're going on trips into the mountains. There aren't any roads – only nature. They call it 'the wilderness' – just woods and heather* and rivers and lakes. There were songs and games after dinner*. It was fun. I hope the weather is better tomorrow.

Wednesday 8th August

I've been here for three days now. We – that's Mary, Sharon and I – arrived together but I feel alone now. Sharon only wants to be with Patrick. She doesn't even listen to us when we say something. She has always got stars* in her eyes*. And Mary spends her time in a different group, with other people. They're quite fun – they laugh all the time. But they aren't really interested in the country. Mary and her new friends don't want to go on the trips or learn about nature. They just want to be on the beach or in the town. I came with two friends and now I haven't got any.

Thursday 9th August

I found a new friend today and now I feel much better. But a new problem comes with my new friend. His name is Ian McCall and he's from Ballymoney. That isn't far from Coleraine. I saw him first in the bus that took us to

the Mourne Mountains. But I didn't speak to him till later – in the mountains. The first words he said to me were, "It's beautiful here, isn't it?" It was. I met him like this.

We had our first long walk in the Mourne Mountains today. Mary and Sharon didn't come. They were in another group again. They like water sports, they say. Well, they like the people who like water sports. Our group only had ten people in it. Four boys, five girls and Mr Kennedy, the warden. We started after breakfast when a small bus arrived for us. It took the road towards Hilltown and stopped after half an hour. Our walk into 'the wilderness' started then.

First we left the road and our path went into a little wood. Then we came out of the wood and the path got bigger. We walked on over the heather and then along a small river. And Ian walked next to me. We stayed together all day. He's lovely when he smiles. We could only hear the water in the river and the songs of the birds. That's when Ian said, "It's beautiful here, isn't it?" And it was beautiful in those mountains. One of them is 852 metres high*. That's very high for our country. We saw some lakes and Silent Valley, too.

We walked for two hours and then stopped for our lunch next to a lake. We had sandwiches and drinks with us. There, Mr Kennedy told* us that there are lots of old stories about the Mourne Mountains.
"I can read some to you this evening," he said. But there was a disco this evening, so he couldn't. After lunch we went down* the mountain. The woods were so quiet and calm*. Ian and I walked behind* the others and talked.
He told me about his family. It's really big. He has got four brothers and a sister! His parents are out of work. They haven't got much money and that makes things difficult. He goes to a small school in Ballymoney. He isn't very good at school but he isn't too bad. He likes reading and animals. He's just like everybody else. Except for one thing. He has never had a Protestant friend before. That's the problem. Ian is a Catholic.

Friday 10th August

Today I explored* Kilkeel with Ian. We went into the town. Some of the buildings are hundreds of years old. We looked at the little shops and then went for a walk along Mourne Esplanade*. We met Sharon and Patrick. They were sitting together and looking at the sea. They were holding* hands so I didn't talk to them. We saw Mary and her friends later on the beach. But I didn't want to stay with them either*. It's funny. I only wanted to talk to Ian today. After dinner this evening

Mr Kennedy read us an old story about an Irish leader called Cuchullain who lived near the Mourne Mountains. I sat next to Ian. We held hands and listened. I don't remember much of the story.

Sunday 12th August

I spent all the weekend with Ian. On Saturday there was a trip to Newry. That's the biggest town near here. Today was very warm and we went to the beach with the others. We had our first argument*. Well, it wasn't really an argument. We talked about the troubles* in Northern Ireland. Ian doesn't think that they are ever going to finish. But I'm sure that there is going to be peace* in Northern Ireland. Ian said that peace can never come if the British – he means the British soldiers – don't go home. So I said, "But I am British, too, Ian." And he just answered, "Well, Karen, do you really think there is a future* for us then? Together?"
Ian is a Catholic but that doesn't worry me. I'm sure there's a future for us. Why can't he see that? Why? Why? Why?

Wednesday 15th August

I haven't had time for my diary. This holiday with Ian is great! We can talk about so many things together. He's serious*, but funny, too. Some of the boys here are silly – but Ian isn't. No, Ian is different. He really is.

Thursday 16th August

It's very hard to write today. I've spent all day alone. Ian's father and brother are coming for him tomorrow. I said, "Oh, great! I'd like to meet them." But he doesn't think that's a good idea. "My family isn't British, Karen. They're Irish. They're Catholics. If they know you're a Protestant, they just won't understand." Ian really thinks there is no future for us. He doesn't want to understand. He's the same as his parents. How can there be peace if Protestants and Catholics can never be together? I asked him that. He said, "It's OK here, Karen. On holiday. But at home, well, it isn't going to be the same. We can't be together at home, Karen. They won't let us. It's very sad, I know. But what can we do?" Well, Ian McCall, they aren't going to stop us. We can be together if that's what we both want.

Saturday 18th August

I couldn't write yesterday. I was too sad. I just cried all day. Ian didn't come to breakfast. Then I looked for him and another boy said, "Ian? Oh, he has gone. His dad came for him. He has gone home." He didn't even say 'Goodbye'.

Our bus left at eleven. I sat alone but Sharon sat next to me later. She could see that I was sad. Mary didn't even understand. She was too busy with her new friends. They laughed and shouted all the way to Coleraine. I told Sharon about Ian. She didn't know he was a Catholic. She's sorry but she doesn't really understand either. She said, "Just try to forget him, Karen. If he's a Catholic, it will never work. You know that." I haven't even got his address. I'm never going to see him again! It isn't fair! God, it isn't fair.

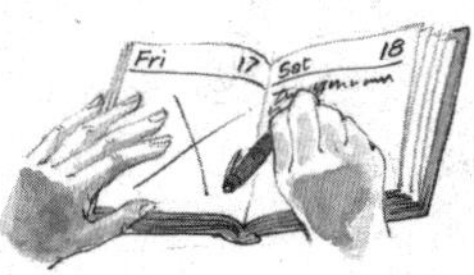

Sunday 19th August

They aren't going to stop us. I told Ian that and I'm right. I know I am. I got up this morning and thought, "I've got to see him again." I felt very calm and I made a plan. It was easy really. I looked in the phone book. Then I started to phone all the McCalls in Ballymoney. I phoned six families. Then I recognised* Ian's voice at once*. He was so surprised – and worried. But I'm going to see him again. We're going to meet in Coleraine next Saturday. He's coming by bus. I think he's happy, too. He said, "My parents mustn't know." And I said, "I've missed you, Ian. Why didn't you say goodbye?" And he said, "I'm sorry, Karen. I'm sorry." And I said, "I've missed you, Ian." And this time he said, "I've missed you, too."
They aren't going to stop us. We can be together. I know we can.

p. 20 diary = *Tagebuch*; Catholic = *Katholik, katholisch*; Republic = *Republik*; Protestant = *Protestant, evangelisch*; lunch = *Mittagessen*; God = *Gott*; let (v) = *lassen, erlauben*
p. 21 sweep down (v) = *hinunterstürzen/-fallen*; beach = *Strand;* heather = *Heidekraut;* dinner = *Abendessen;* star = *Stern;* eye = *Auge*
p. 22 high = *hoch*
p. 23 told (v) = *erzählte;* go down (v) = *hinuntergehen;* calm = *ruhig;* behind = *hinter;* explore (v) = *erkunden;* esplanade = *Promenade;* hold (v) = *halten;* either = *auch nicht*
p. 24 argument = *Streit;* troubles = *Schwierigkeiten, Probleme;* peace = *Frieden;* future = *Zukunft ;* serious = *ernst*
p. 26 recognise (v) = *erkennen;* at once = *sofort*

Orkney adventure

When dad came home from Dundee that day in June and explained about the boat, it was a real* surprise for my brother Alexander and me. Our grandfather died in May and the boat was his – the 'Silver Spray'.

"A boat! We're boat owners!" I said. "When can we go out in it?"
Dad already had an idea. "What about a trip to the Orkney Islands*?" he said. "In July, when school has finished for the summer holidays?" Dad's plan was a three-hundred-mile journey along the coast from Dundee up to John O'Groats and then to the Orkney Islands.
"How fast can the 'Silver Spray' go?" we wanted to know.
"About ten miles per hour," said Dad. "We can travel six hours a day, so we can do the trip in ten or twelve days. I love the Orkney Islands. I visited them with your grandad when I was a boy."

Alex and I liked the idea, but mum didn't want to come with us.
"The boat is too small for four. I know, Kirstie. I've already been on it," she said to me. "And I don't really like the sea much." I talked to her for a long time but she still said 'no'.

On the first day of the holiday, mum drove* us all to the Firth of Tay, the big river in Dundee. Grandad always left his boat there. The 'Silver Spray' was a beautiful name but the boat didn't look very beautiful; the yellow paint was dirty and it was difficult to read the name. We towed* the boat to the river and tied it up with a rope.

We all fetched some clean water and we cleaned everything on the boat. "This isn't my idea of a holiday!" said Alex, but it was only a joke. He enjoyed the work, I think. Then dad started the engine*. It coughed and there was lots of black smoke* but after a few minutes the engine ran very well. We worked all day and finished work at six pm. We couldn't start our journey that day because the work took so long. Mum left that evening and we spent the first night of our holiday in the boat on the River Tay. At last we were on the water, even if we were still in Dundee.

Next morning, we got up with the sun. It was a beautiful morning. At half past seven we were ready and dad started the engine. There wasn't very much smoke this time. We travelled under the bridge over the Firth of Tay to the sea. People were just going to work.

For five days we travelled along the coast of Scotland. Every evening we stopped at a harbour* for the night. Alex wanted to listen to the weather reports and talk to the other ships on the boat's radio, but we only had a receiver* and it was very old. Some of the time it didn't work.

After five days, we arrived in John O'Groats, only ten miles from the Orkney Islands. The next morning we started from John O'Groats at nine am.

"It's going to take about two hours. There are strong currents* here," dad said. At eleven o'clock we saw the Orkney Islands. We travelled past lots of smaller islands in Scapa Flow. At last, at one o'clock we saw the island of Mainland and soon arrived at the town of Stromness. The grey houses of Stromness are about 250 years old. The streets are full of tourists in the summer. "I don't remember any tourists when I came here with your grandfather," dad said. He wanted to buy a present for mum so he went to look at the shops.

Alex and I stayed in the harbour and looked at the fishing boats. We were looking at a nice red fishing boat, when two men in oilskins* arrived.

"Hallo, you two!" said one of the men. "Do you like our boat?" They were really friendly.

"Very much," I said.

"I'm John MacGregor and this is my brother Bennie. Are you brother and sister?"

"Yes, we are," said Alex. "That's our boat," he said and pointed to the 'Silver Spray'.

"Well, that's a nice little boat for a holiday. But it isn't very good for the sea round here. The sea runs fast here and the currents can be dangerous," said John.

"We don't know much about the sea or about boats," I said.

"What do you do in an emergency*? Do you know?" asked John. We said 'no', so John MacGregor took us into the cabin*. He put a book on the table.

"These are the emergency signals," he explained. "Look at them and learn them." He showed us a picture of them in the book.

"We know all the dangerous currents and the difficult sandbanks here. We've got to know them. The difficult places are often the best places for fish," said Bennie. "There's a good place for fish near Switha. It can be dangerous for small boats in bad weather. But there's a safe harbour there. We often go there. We'll be there tomorrow," he said. Then he showed us the place on his map. Bennie made some tea and we talked for a time.

That evening, we played cards with dad on our boat and then we phoned mum from the telephone in the harbour.

"This is a great holiday!" we said. "Please come next time." Mum agreed to think about it. Next morning, we started on our journey back to John O'Groats. The weather wasn't so nice now. It was very cloudy and windy.

"Can you get a weather forecast, Alex?" dad said. Alex tried the radio in the cabin but it didn't work. Soon we were in Scapa Flow and the boat was rolling* from left to right. I felt quite sick for a few minutes. Near the island of Hoy the sea was really rough*. It started to rain. I took dad his oilskins from the cabin. Suddenly, Alex shouted,

"Dad, the radio is working again!" He had to shout because it was so windy.
"We're going to have a gale*!"
"What did you say?" said dad. "I can't hear you!"
"A gale! We're going to have a gale!" said Alex.
"It's already here!" shouted dad. "Don't worry," he said, but he was worried. "We've got to try to find a safe harbour," he said. "The sea is too rough for us. Our engine isn't strong enough."
"There's a safe place near Switha," I said. "Those fishermen showed us on their map."
"Good girl!" said dad. "Can you bring me our map?" He looked at it for a time and then he said, "We'll go past South Walls to that harbour. We'll be safe there." Alex and I went into the cabin out of the rain. We made dad a cup of coffee because it was very cold outside at the steering-wheel*. Dad smiled at me, but he was very white.

After twenty minutes, he called to us, "We're going past South Walls now. It won't be long now. We'll see the harbour soon." We looked out of the windows and couldn't see anything except the rain. Our small boat was rolling and jumping in the rough sea.

Suddenly, the boat stopped with a terrible noise. We both fell on to the floor and dad fell into the cabin and his stomach hit* the table.

"Dad!" shouted Alex. "Are you all right?" Dad was in a lot of pain.

"We're aground*," he said. "Probably a sandbank. Can you see anything?" Alex went on to deck and quickly returned.

"Yes, it **is** a sandbank. We're aground. And the steering-wheel is broken," said Alex. He was frightened.

"But the coast is miles away," I said.

"Not miles, but about half a mile," said dad. "Too far. We can't swim in this sea."

"What can we do, Dad?" said Alex.

"We'll have to wait," said dad. "Perhaps another ship will see us." But there wasn't another ship near us. The 'Silver Spray' was still upright* on the sandbank. But for how long? The sea was very rough. We couldn't call for help. Dad was white and very ill. We were all wet and cold.

"We've got to do something," Alex said to me. "But what?"

"We need an emergency signal. Perhaps somebody will see us. Let's look in the cupboards," I said. I opened a cupboard. There was only one flag in there – a Scottish flag.

"We can't use that!" said Alex.

"How can we show an emergency signal without the right flags?" I asked.

"No, it's all right!" Alex shouted. "The signal for 'I'm aground' is almost the same as the Scottish flag! Remember?"

"You're right. We'll use it. I'll do it," said Alex, and I was glad. I didn't want to climb on deck in that weather.

I tied a rope round Alex. He climbed on to the deck and almost fell into the sea. Then he raised* the flag on the mast. It was very dangerous. Soon the flag was flying on the mast.

"Well done, Alex!" I shouted.

"Now we just have to wait – and hope," dad said. We sat in the cabin with dad and drank coffee. It felt like hours.

The angry wind hit the 'Silver Spray' again and again and three times the boat moved* suddenly. I thought, "This is the end," but our small boat stayed upright. Alex tried the radio again but it didn't work. "How long is this gale going to last*?" I thought. There was lots of water on the cabin floor. We sang some songs and we felt better for a time. But soon we stopped singing. Dad looked at us. I could see he had a terrible pain in his stomach.

"I'm sorry," he said. "This holiday was a silly idea."

Suddenly, there was a noise outside.

"What was that?" I said. There was the noise again. Alex and I ran outside. There was a light and we could see a boat about fifty metres away.

"Can it see us? Is it coming this way?" Alex said. We shouted.

"Yes, it's coming this way," I shouted. "It has seen us!"

It only took a minute and the other boat was fifteen metres away. There was a man on deck and he shouted something but we couldn't hear what he said. Then he showed us a rope.

"I understand," I said. "He's going to throw the rope."

The man threw* the rope but it fell into the sea.

"He's too far away!" Alex said.

"Yes, but if he comes nearer, he'll be aground, too!" I shouted. But the other boat came nearer. It was only five metres away now.

"He's too near!" shouted Alex. "He'll hit us!"

Then the man threw the wet rope again. This time it fell on our deck. Alex and I tied it on to the 'Silver Spray'. We shouted. The man shouted, too. We went into the cabin. It was safer there. Then the other boat pulled. At first, nothing happened, then suddenly the 'Silver Spray' was free!

"He's done it!" we shouted.

"What's happening?" dad asked. "What's that noise?"

"It's OK, Dad. Another boat is rescuing us!" I said.

"Thank goodness!" he said and smiled. The journey to the nearest safe harbour took almost half an hour. At last we arrived. We could see the other boat better now. It was a nice red fishing boat. There was a man on deck.

"Hallo, Alex! Hallo, Kirstie! So you learned your emergency signals. Well done!" he shouted. It was Bennie MacGregor.

p. 27 real = *echt;* island = *Insel;* drove (v) = *fuhr;* tow (v) = *schleppen*

p. 28 engine = *Motor;* smoke = *Rauch;* harbour = *Hafen;* receiver = *Empfänger*

p. 29 current = *Strömung;* oilskins = *Ölkleidung;* emergency = *Notfall;* cabin = *Kajüte*

p. 30 roll (v) = *schaukeln;* rough = *stürmisch*

p. 31 gale = *Sturm;* steering-wheel = *Steuerrad*

p. 32 hit (v) = *schlagen gegen, zusammenstoßen mit;* aground = *gestrandet;* upright = *aufrecht*

p. 33 raise (v) = *hissen;* move (v) = *sich bewegen;* last (v) = *(an)dauern;* threw (v)= *warf*

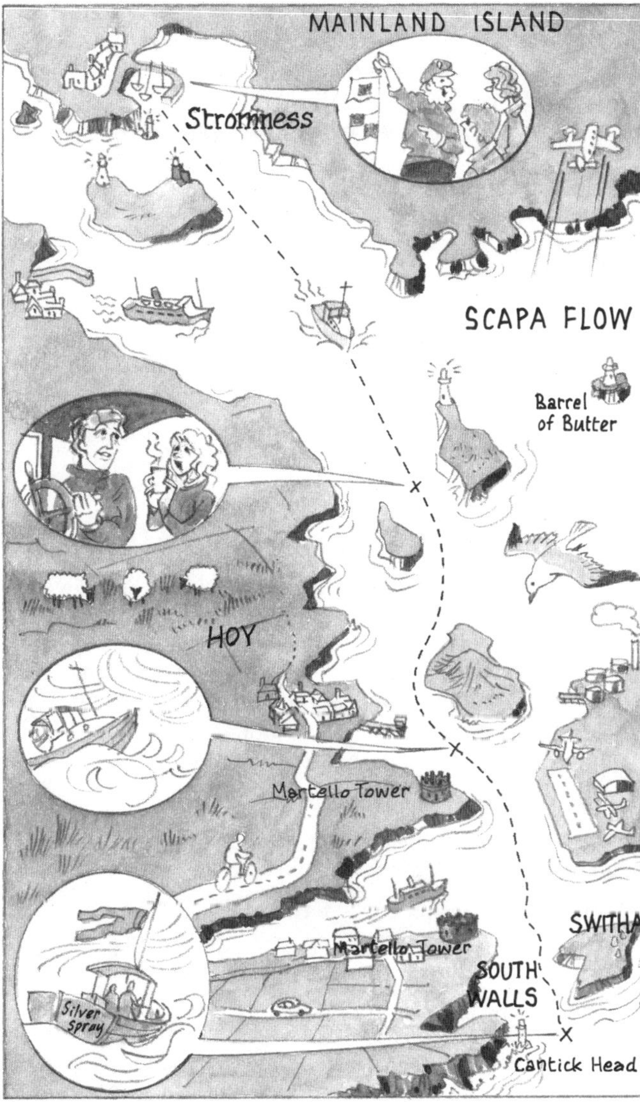
MAINLAND ISLAND
Stromness
SCAPA FLOW
Barrel of Butter
HOY
Martello Tower
Martello Tower
SWITHA
SOUTH WALLS
Silver Spray
Cantick Head

After the stories ...

The Kingfisher

A How many words can you make from BIRD-WATCHERS?
Try to write 12 words in five minutes.
Example: ride

B Make a list of all the words that have to do with a nature reserve. Compare your list with a partner's list.

C Find the words. The letters in boxes give you another word from the text.

1. Jessica tried to ---❑ -- the kingfisher.
2. Suddenly they heard another --❑--.
3. They made a ❑--- for the bird.
4. There was a ❑---- of children.
5. The kingfisher didn't ❑-- away.
6. Chris doesn't want to talk to -❑---- children.
7. There are a lot of --❑--- in the nature reserve.
8. They walked along the ---❑ at Breydon Water.
9. The kingfisher had a nice blue -❑--.
10. There were lots of birds in the ----❑.

D Make a poster for a nature reserve. Write about:
when it's open,
what animals you can see there,
what else you can do there,
the warden who shows tourists around etc.

E Have you ever been to a nature reserve? Think of all the things you can do there. Make a plan for one day.

The hard way up

A Find all the words in the text that have to do with a survival holiday.

B Write all the things you need for a survival holiday. You can also look them up in a German-English dictionary.

C Chain Game.
The first pupil says, "For a survival holiday I need a rucksack."
The second pupil says, "For a survival holiday I need a rucksack and a tent." Go on.

D What things can you do when you go on a survival holiday? Work with a partner. Make a plan for three days. Compare your plans.

E Scrambled words. The letters in boxes give you another word from the text.

1. In the tent they find shelter from the **di[n]w**.
2. The children have to sleep in **s[t]net**.
3. The name of one of the children is **ry[b]ar**.
4. Each child has to carry a **kacs[k]ucr**.
5. The children try to find a good place for a **p[a]mc.**
6. The leaders have to know all the survival **sli[l]sk.**
7. The tents are very **vyah[e]** to carry.

F Write an advert for a survival tour for young people between 12 and 18. Write about the place, the time and the cost.

They aren't going to stop us

A Find nine words from the text.

TKAGREEPNWZYLUNCHAQPONVUTWILDERNESSTH
YMCHJNUIORWNDINNERLKWQPODNSTARASPPJYM
UZTJJGFHTROUBLESNYXCPIINFSDIARYQWLION
HGFJIBEACHALSNDTIUARGUMENTLKQOWUYDKLN

B Find out about all the activities you can do at a holiday camp.
Make a list. Work with a partner. Make a plan for one day.
Compare your plans.

C Complete the sentences. Put the letters in boxes into the right order. They give you a word from the text.

1. Karen is going to spend two weeks at a -❑--.
2. Mary spends her time in a different -❑---.
3. After some days Karen finds a --❑---.
4. Together they go for long --❑--.
5. In the evenings they sit and hold --❑--.
6. Karen loves writing her ❑----.
7. At home she tries to find Ian's name in the ---- ❑----.

D In her diary Karen writes about the problems of Protestants and Catholics.
Find these problems in the text.
What do **you** know about these problems?

E Look at 'Sunday 19th August'. Work with a partner and make a dialogue of Karen's telephone call to Ian.

Orkney adventure

A Find all the things in the text you have and/or need on a boat.

B Word snake. The last letter of one word is the first letter of the next word

1. On board the boat there was only a ...
2. It's much better to have a good ...
3. They're planning a trip to the ...
4. When they first start there's a lot of ...
5. The ... is very old.
6. Every ... they stopped at a harbour.
7. A ... is another word for a bad storm.

C Look at a map of Scotland. Find the towns that are in the text. Describe the trip.

D Scrambled words. They all have to do with the emergency.

lega, gruoh, lianisg, kisc, dyniw, poer, nadskanb, glaf.

Put the words in the right order. Talk about the family's emergency
or
write a report for a newspaper.

E Make a weather report for the day of the emergency. Give information about *rain, wind, gale, clouds, temperatures.*
Work with a partner. Compare your weather reports.

F Do you think it was a good idea for the father to take his children on a holiday in an old small boat?

List of names

Alexander [ælɪg'zɑːndə]
Ballymoney [bælɪ'mʌnɪ]
Barry ['bærɪ]
Bennie ['benɪ]
Breydon Water ['breɪdən 'wɔːtə]
Clive [klaɪv]
Coleraine [kəʊl'reɪn]
Cuchullain ['kuːkʊlɪn]
Dundee [dʌn'diː]
Firth of Tay ['fɜːθ əv 'teɪ]
Gateway ['geɪtweɪ]
Great Yarmouth [greɪt 'jɑːməθ]
Hickling Broad ['hɪklɪŋ 'brɔːd]
Jed [dʒed]
Jessica ['dʒesɪkə]
John O' Groats [dʒɒnə'grəʊts]
Kennedy ['kenɪdɪ]
Kilkeel [kɪl'kiːl]
Kirstie ['kɜːstɪ]
Lisburn ['lɪzbɜːn]
MacGregor [mə'gregə]
Mainland ['meɪnlənd]
McCall [mə'kɔːl]
McFee [mək'fiː]
Mourne Mountains ['mɔːn 'maʊntɪnz]
Newry ['njʊərɪ]
Nicole [nɪ'kɒl]
Norfolk Broads ['nɔːfək 'brɔːdz]
Orkney Islands ['ɔːknɪ aɪləndz]
Patrick ['pætrɪk]
Porthmadog [pɔːθ'mædɒg]
River Tay [rɪvə 'teɪ]
Scapa Flow [skæpə 'fləʊ]
Sharon ['ʃærən]
Silent Valley ['saɪlənt 'vælɪ]
Silver Spray ['sɪlvə 'spreɪ]
Snowdon ['snəʊdn]
Sonia ['sɒnɪə]
South Walls [saʊθ 'wɔːlz]
Stromness ['strɒmnes]
Sutton ['sʌtn]
Switha ['swɪðə]
Wentworth ['wentwəθ]